D0616210

MAKE
THEIR
DAY

MAKE THEIR DAY

101 Simple, Powerful Ways to *Love Others Well*

KAREN EHMAN

BETHANYHOUSE

a division of Baker Publishing Group
Minneapolis, Minnesota

© 2021 by Karen Ehman

Published by Bethany House Publishers
11400 Hampshire Avenue South
Bloomington, Minnesota 55438
www.bethanyhouse.com

Bethany House Publishers is a division of
Baker Publishing Group, Grand Rapids, Michigan

Printed in the United States of America

Library of Congress Control Number: 2020046027

ISBN 978-0-7642-3842-0 (paperback)
ISBN 978-0-7642-3904-5 (casebound)
ISBN 978-1-4934-3162-5 (ebook)

Unless otherwise indicated, Scripture quotations have been taken from the Christian Standard Bible®, copyright © 2017 by Holman Bible Publishers. Used by permission. Christian Standard Bible® and CSB® are federally registered trademarks of Holman Bible Publishers.

Scripture quotations identified CEB are from the Common English Bible. © Copyright 2011 by the Common English Bible. All rights reserved. Used by permission.

Scripture quotations identified ESV are from The Holy Bible, English Standard Version® (ESV®), copyright © 2001 by Crossway, a publishing ministry of Good News Publishers. Used by permission. All rights reserved. ESV Text Edition: 2016

Scripture quotations identified NIV are from THE HOLY BIBLE, NEW INTERNATIONAL VERSION®, NIV® Copyright © 1973, 1978, 1984, 2011 by Biblica, Inc.® Used by permission. All rights reserved worldwide.

Scripture quotations identified NLT are taken from the Holy Bible, New Living Translation, copyright © 1996, 2004, 2015 by Tyndale House Foundation. Used by permission of Tyndale House Publishers, Inc., Carol Stream, Illinois 60188. All rights reserved.

Cover design by Emily Weigel

21 22 23 24 25 26 27   7 6 5 4 3 2 1

To Aunt Susie

For the 101 ways that knowing you
makes me smile

Contents

Introduction   9

PART ONE
In Your Circle of Friends   11

PART TWO
Within Your Own Family   27

PART THREE
Throughout Your Day and around the Town   43

PART FOUR
Across the Miles or through the Screen   55

PART FIVE

For Those Who Hurt or Need Help   67

PART SIX

Among the Household of Faith   83

PART SEVEN

On Holidays, Holy Days, or Just Because   97

PART EIGHT

By Opening Your Home   119

Printables   131

Introduction

Let us consider each other carefully for the purpose of
sparking love and good deeds.

Hebrews 10:24 CEB

Ever grow weary of all the bad news? Each time we flip on the
evening broadcast, we hear of more turmoil, unrest, poverty,
sickness, and devastation. Escaping to social media doesn't
paint any prettier of a picture. There, our eyes witness a nearly
constant scroll of snark and sarcasm—at best. At worst, we
see the outright hurling of hate.

While complaining to my husband recently about all the
ugliness I see, I became convicted that my irritation spilling
out verbally really accomplishes nothing. Nothing at all. Perhaps I need to stop talking and start acting instead.

In 1907, William Lonsdale Watkinson, an English Wes-
leyan minister, said something that has been repeated over
the years by others, most notably by President John F. Ken-
nedy. The pastor asserted, "Denunciatory rhetoric is so much

easier and cheaper than good works, and proves a popular temptation. Yet is it far better to light the candle than to curse the darkness."*

Yes! That's it. *We need to be lighting candles.*

This little book is full of 101 simple yet powerful ideas that I pray will—in the spirit of Hebrews 10:24—spark some love and spur on some good deeds. Consider this your go-to guide as you scatter kindness and shower love on friends, family, faraway loved ones, and even strangers. Let's do our part in outshining the negativity and hatred. Not so others will look at us and think we are oh-so-humanitarian and utterly amazing, but so they will think of God.

> "In the same way, let your light shine before others, that they may see your good deeds and glorify your Father in heaven."
>
> Matthew 5:16 NIV

It's time we stopped cursing the darkness. Go grab a candle. I'll snatch one too. Together, we can count on God to provide us with a spiritual spark that will enable us to show to the watching world his goodness and glory.

In Jesus,

Karen

---

*W[illiam] L[onsdale] Watkinson, "The Invincible Strategy," in *The Supreme Conquest, and Other Sermons Preached in America* (New York: Fleming H. Revell, 1907), 217–218, https://archive.org/details/supremeconquesto00watk.

PART ONE

In Your Circle of Friends

Encourage one another and build each other up as you are already doing.

1 THESSALONIANS 5:11

Try any one of these ideas—some simple, some more involved—to lovingly say, "Thank you for being a friend!"

1.

A surprise coffee delivery

There's nothing better for a little pick-me-up than a fresh cup of coffee. In order to surprise a friend on a day she might need cheering—or simply to let her know she is seen and loved—show up to her home or place of work with her favorite signature drink from a local coffee shop.

In order to make sure that her beverage is prepared exactly as she likes it, the next time the two of you are out to a coffeehouse, listen carefully when she places her custom order. Then document it in the Notes app on your phone. Then you will be able to surprise her with her preferred drink. I did this for a friend on the day after her only child moved away to college. I knew it would be an emotional day for her, so I delivered a steaming mug of caramel mocha—made extra hot, with skim milk and light whip—to her home. She had no idea how I knew what she liked until I revealed that I had saved it in my phone.

2.

Team up to tackle a chore

Chores. We all have them. And many times, we hate doing them. Whether it is cleaning out the junk drawer and messy closets in your home, or tackling an overdue DIY project, such as stripping wallpaper from the bathroom walls before covering them in a fresh coat of paint, doing these tasks alone certainly is no fun.

Using card stock, photocopy the Choose-a-Chore coupon found on page 132 to give to a friend for one two-hour session, or perhaps one entire Saturday, of chore assistance. Your friend names the chore. You will show up, ready to help tackle it. Be sure to fill in the expiration date and the phone number where your friend can text the code "Free Help" in order to redeem the coupon.

On the day your friend chooses, you show up to assist in tackling the task. Bring along a snack and a thermos of something to drink so you can take a break to refresh yourselves. She will be so thankful not only to have the chore behind her, but also to have such a good friend alongside her in life.

3.

Get creative and crafty

For a clever present for a friend, register the two of you for a creative and crafty afternoon of art. There are several options to choose from. You could register to paint on canvas in a beginner's class. You could sign up to make and glaze a piece of pottery, such as a mug or serving bowl. There may even be places in your area that teach hand-lettering or jewelry making. Find a day that works for both you and your friend. Then, pick her up for the class and, once it is over, treat her to lunch. Using the creative part of your brain not only can be relaxing, but also helps to rejuvenate your mind, making you ready to get back into life and tackle it with gusto.

4.

You get my message?

Send a message—literally—to a friend, letting her know how much she means to you. Purchase a personal-sized message board, the type that has a felt background with grooves embedded in it and comes with precut plastic letters that can be used to make messages. Spell out a message such as "Thank you for being a friend" or "A friend loves at all times (Proverbs 17:17)," and then wrap up the board for gifting. This gift will not only deliver a sentiment, but will be a playful decorative item for her home. Many people also use these to stage pictures for social media.

5.

Throw a surprise slumber party

For my thirtieth birthday, my husband arranged for two friends to stage a kidnapping that resulted in one of my most treasured memories. I thought I was going out to a celebratory dinner with my husband. Instead, two friends rushed into my house dressed in pajamas and bathrobes, with curlers in their hair. (One even used small frozen orange juice containers for her curlers!) They made me change into my pajamas, put a blindfold on my eyes, and then whisked me away in their getaway vehicle. I had no idea what was happening.

Once we arrived at the destination, I was guided, still blind-folded, into the building. Things were very quiet. But when they told me I could remove my blindfold, I heard a chorus of voices shouting, "Surprise!" I nearly fell over. Thirty friends, also dressed in their sleepwear, were at my church in a room with sleeping bags spread all over. There were crazy skits, goofy games, pepperoni pizzas, and other assorted snacks. Several friends had even gotten together to rehearse a cheer they made up, all about me: "Karen, Karen, heart of gold! Too bad she is (clap, clap) so old!"

Think about a friend who would be blessed with a surprise slumber party. Tailor the celebration to her liking. At the time mine was held, I was a cheerleading coach and youth group leader, so my party ran along those two themes. Of course, you will need somebody to pretend they are actually taking this person out to dinner or an evening movie so that you will be sure she is available. Such a hoot and so very sneaky!

6.

Host a sorta-spa party

Are you a bit worn-out? Got any frazzled friends? Plan a time of rest, relaxation, and refreshment for all of you by hosting a sorta-spa party. Complete with facials, manicures, chocolate, prayer, and reflection, this will renew your spirits and settle your souls. Here are the steps to throwing this pampering party.

Photocopy and then send out the invitations provided on page 133.

Gather the following ingredients for the party:

- A package of hypoallergenic makeup wipes.

- Tubes of cucumber or charcoal face masks. Be sure to take into account different skin types—dry, oily, sensitive—when purchasing.

- A few candles scented with relaxing essential oils. Good choices are lavender, eucalyptus, lemongrass, or peppermint. You can also use an oil diffuser if you'd rather not burn candles.

- Some jars of sugar scrub.

- A tube of rich, thick, scented hand cream. (My favorite is the rose oil one from Trader Joe's!)

- Some nail files and bottles of nail polish in various colors.

- Assorted chocolates or even chocolate-dipped fresh strawberries.

- A few pitchers of ice water. Flavor them by adding in lightly crushed slices of cucumber; wedges of lemon and lime; fresh basil, mint, or rosemary leaves; or fresh blackberries or raspberries.

- For those who would like a hot drink, set up a coffee and tea bar with some rock sugar, assorted creamers, and bags of tea.

- Some relaxing, instrumental worship music ready to go on your device or sound system.

- Chilled slices of cucumbers and enough washcloths for each person.

- If desired, a copy for each guest of *Settle My Soul: 100 Quiet Moments to Meet with Jesus* by Ruth Schwenk and Karen Ehman. Tie a pretty coordinating ribbon around each book and be sure to sign the dedication page to each person.

Prepare your home for a time of restful relaxation by lighting lots of candles (or starting the oil diffusers) and lowering the lights. Provide plenty of comfortable seating and have the music playing softly. Place the chocolates in dishes around the room.

About two hours before the start time, place the washcloths, dampened slightly with water, in a Crock-Pot on low heat and place the lid on. When guests arrive, gather together and welcome them. Tell them your desire is for them to have a few hours to relax and clear their minds. You may want to begin the time with prayer or by reading a short devotion on rest. Then the relaxing begins!

Have the women remove their makeup with the makeup wipes. Then they can each put on their masks and relax for several minutes while the masks work their magic. They can also place cucumber slices on their eyes if they desire. After about fifteen minutes, they can use the warmed damp washcloths to remove the masks from their faces.

Next, instead of an actual foot-washing ceremony, have the women pair up and take turns scrubbing each other's hands with the sugar scrub, rinsing them in a sink, and then massaging them with the scented hand lotion. Consider it a holy hand rub! If you would like, the person doing the scrubbing and applying the lotion can pray out loud for the woman on the receiving end.

Next, the guests can either choose a bottle of nail polish and paint their own nails, or they can paint each other's nails. Be sure to take breaks to enjoy a beverage or some of the chocolates. If you desire to take this party up a notch, you could even provide snacks or a light lunch.

When your time is over, send each guest off with her copy of *Settle My Soul* or another small gift, such as a tube of hand cream, scented candle, or journal and pen. What a fun way to show love to your friends by giving them a little respite from life!

7.

Time-travel to shop for a nostalgic pick-me-up

For a clever gift for a friend, do a little nosing around. See if you can discover something nostalgic from her childhood that evokes fond memories for her. Then, visit an online auction site, such as eBay, to see if you can locate the item to purchase.

I once found a particular small, chunky hardcover book a friend of mine remembered from her childhood. She recalls taking it off her grandmother's shelf often when she would visit, and curling up on the couch to read it. When she told me that story one day, I jotted the title of the book down in my Notes app so I would not forget. She was thrilled when she opened her gift and didn't even remember telling me that story. Other items that are fun to discover from someone's childhood are board games, vintage magazines with their most-loved teenage heartthrob on the cover, retro toys, or trendy objects. (Think anything from Troll dolls to Strawberry Shortcake, Tamagotchis to Sky Dancers!)

8.

Become a Bible-reading buddy

Do you have a friend who has mentioned that she wishes she was more consistent in her Bible reading? Here's a simple idea to help her—and also yourself—read the Bible on a more consistent basis.

Purchase two copies of a one-year chronological Bible. This type of Bible divides the text into 365 readings, and has the content laid out in the historic order that the events occurred or that the content was written.

Give one copy to your friend, along with a little note suggesting that the two of you can hold each other accountable to read the Bible every day. You might want to adopt the habit of simply texting each other once you have read the entry for the day—of course, accompanied with loads of grace for the inevitable days when you won't get it finished. It can help both of you keep on track when you decide to partner together to read God's Word.

Note: One-year chronological Bibles begin with January 1, but you could easily adapt them to start any time of the year by just beginning at the front of the Bible and reading one entry per day.

9.

It takes two

Do you have a friend who could use a little getaway from—or perhaps some adventure in—her life? Invite her to partake in an activity with you that requires two people. It could be a leisurely trip down a lazy river in a canoe or kayak built for two. Or perhaps you can take in a relaxing ride on a rented tandem bike as you meander through a large park or nature center, stopping to eat a picnic lunch. If something more fast-paced is up your alley, rent go-karts or even dune buggies, if you have a sandy beach in your area where that activity is popular.

When your excursion is done, keep with the "it takes two" theme as you seek out a little refreshment. Perhaps use a buy-one-get-one-free coupon at a coffeehouse or ice-cream shop. Or treat your friend to a You Pick Two meal at Panera Bread or a similar deal at a restaurant where she gets to choose two items from a luncheon menu such as soup and salad or soup and half a sandwich.

10.

Give a lovely Bible-time teacup bundle

Super easy to assemble and oh-so-pretty! Purchase a new Bible or a devotional book. Next, on top of it, place a teacup and saucer (new or from a resale or antique store). In the cup place a few bags of tea. Tie it all up with a large square of pretty tulle (netting) and secure with some satin ribbon in a coordinating color, fastening it in a big bow on top. Slip an antique teaspoon in the knot of the bow. Your friend can use the items in her time alone with God. You can include a copy of the tag on page 140 featuring Psalm 105:4 (CEB), "Pursue the Lord and his strength; seek his face always!"

11.

Give the starter for a loaf of friendship bread

A friend once gave me some sourdough starter in an antique mason jar, along with a handwritten recipe for a loaf of delicious bread using the starter. I've been hooked on sourdough ever since!

Typically, you must keep feeding the sourdough starter, grabbing some out to make a loaf of bread or to divide with a friend. Today, you can purchase sourdough starter online. (I use Breadtopia Sourdough Starter found on Amazon.com.) Order yourself a small package of it and let the baking begin!

Once your starter arrives, feed it according to directions. When you get enough to give some to a friend, place one cup of it in a whimsical or antique jar with a lid. Give it to your friend, along with the instructions for feeding the starter and the recipe for making a loaf of sourdough bread found on page 134. Encourage your friend to keep the love going by gifting another friend with her own starter in a jar.

12.

Say it with candy

Send a sweet—and somewhat sassy—message using candy and make a friend smile. I first did this for my friend Todd in college. (He later became my husband!)

Purchase a piece of poster board. Then, go to your local candy aisle to purchase several candy bars and other assorted confections whose names will help you create a one-of-a-kind message. You will simply use colored permanent markers to write out your sentiment, leaving spaces to fasten the candy to the poster board. (You can affix them with duct tape rolled on the backs of the candy.) Here's an example:

Please don't label me a "Nerd" and "Snicker" at me for this message. Since you are such a "SweeTART" and I adore you to "Reese's Pieces," I wanted to take some "Extra" time to wish you "Mounds" of "Almond Joy" today. I felt like I hit the jackpot with a "Payday" of "100 Grand" the day you became my friend. So "Take 5" and enjoy a treat from me. Your friendship is truly a "Life Saver."

Hugs and "Hershey Kisses,"
Your Friend, Karen

13.

Give the gift of listening

To encourage a friend, give her the gift of listening—listening to podcasts and books, that is!

Compile a list of your favorite encouraging podcasts. They may be ones on spiritual growth, or they may be just-for-fun ones that have to do with cooking, home decorating, or DIY projects. They could even be humorous or history-themed. Craft an email with the links to all of these podcasts. In it, also include a digital gift card in the proper amount to purchase a one- or two-month subscription to an audiobook site such as Scribd, Kobo, Libro.fm, Audible, or ChristianAudio. Send her the email, along with a message letting her know you want her to experience some audible encouragement while she is walking, doing housework, or commuting.

PART TWO

Within Your
Own Family

Look at how good and pleasing it is when families live together as one!

PSALM 133:1 CEB

Truth be told, our immediate family members sometimes get the brunt of our bad behavior. Instead of grumpiness, sprinkle a little kindness around your place with any of these ideas designed to delight your family members.

14.

Shower the people you love with love

This is a tradition we have typically done on someone's birthday, but you could try it anytime. You might even want to do it on a half birthday, which is six months to the day on the calendar year. (Those late-December babies get tired of competing with Christmas, ya know. They'd love to celebrate a half birthday in June!)

Here's how it works: Everyone in attendance takes a turn sharing one characteristic they really appreciate about the person being showered or one memory that stands out and attests to what kind of person he or she is. You might say, "I love how fiercely loyal Kaley is to her friends and family." Or I might mention the time it was evident what a tenderhearted and kind person my husband is when, as we were walking into a restaurant, he stopped to help a man who was trying to cross a snowy street in his wheelchair but kept getting stuck.

In addition to the showering of love, allow the person being encouraged to set the menu for the night, whether it is a homemade chicken potpie or subs from a favorite sandwich shop.

15.

Give God's Holy Word along with your written words of nostalgia and encouragement

This is a beautiful gift to give to a daughter but could be adapted for anyone you love. Purchase a wide-margin Bible. They are often called journaling Bibles or note-taking Bibles. At least a year before gifting your Bible for a birthday, graduation, or other special occasion, read through the Bible, making notes in the margins as you do. You might tell how a particular verse was one you clung to when your child was younger. You might point out something you learned about another passage or mention that a certain section of the Bible is a prayer you are currently praying for the recipient. When she opens her gift, not only will she be receiving a brand-new Bible, but it will be full of nostalgic memories and encouraging messages in your very own handwriting. What a treasured gift!

16.

Send some lunchtime love

So many of our daytime hours are spent away from those we love the most. How can you reach out when the children are at school or your spouse eats lunch at an office many miles away?

Try this: Pack some unconventional love notes inside their lunches. Get creative! Write "I'm bananas for you" in Sharpie on the banana peel and tuck it in your child's lunch. Or, with a ballpoint pen, write "Even though we drive each other nuts, I'm glad I married you" on a napkin that accompanies a bag of cashews or almonds placed in your spouse's meal. Or, place a sticky note with an encouraging message inside your teen's sandwich container lid on the day of a final exam, secured alongside a favorite candy bar.

17.

Hold a modern-day foot washing

One Mother's Day, my husband organized a beautiful gift for me from my three children. He had us all meet together in the living room and seated me in a comfortable chair with the rest of the family around me. Then, he brought in a basin of warm soapy water, accompanied by a washcloth, a fluffy bath towel, and a tube of lemon-mint lotion.

One by one, my children took turns with the washcloth, gently cleansing my feet with the soapy water. Then they dried my feet off with the bath towel and took turns rubbing the aromatic lotion into my feet. As they massaged my feet, they also told me one thing they loved about me being their mom. My eyes began to leak as I heard their caring words. It was my favorite Mother's Day ever.

18.

Assemble a book basket

This is a themed idea that is so versatile and always a hit! The first time I saw this fantastic idea was when my daughter received a Laura Ingalls Wilder book basket when she was about seven. In it was a vintage hardcover copy of *Little House in the Big Woods*. The basket included several items Laura got for Christmas in the early 1870s as described in that book as well as in Wilder's later book *Little House on the Prairie*.

- a peppermint stick
- a pair of red mittens
- a rag doll named Charlotte
- her own tin cup
- a heart-shaped cake sprinkled with white sugar
- a shiny new penny

It was such a clever gift because it encouraged my daughter to read the book so she could play with all of the items in the basket.

In the years since, I have given away lots of book baskets to children in our extended family. Some books I have used are *Mr. Popper's Penguins*, *The Tale of Peter Rabbit*, and *Winnie-the-Pooh*. The Curious George books are also great for this. In one book, he visits a candy factory. In another, he takes a trip to the zoo. In yet another, he makes pancakes. It's easy to come up with items to carry out the theme—fancy chocolates, candy molds, and supplies; animal crackers, gummy bears, and a stuffed animal; pancake mix, turner, maple syrup, and chocolate chips.

Don't stop with the children. You can also pick out a book for an adult in your family and round out a theme basket as well. For that relative who lives in a Southern state, maybe gift a new Southern cookbook, along with a wooden spoon, a new red-checkered kitchen towel, some Carolina barbecue sauce, creole mustard, and Tabasco sauce. Don't forget to tuck in a bag of buttermilk biscuit mix!

19.

Here comes the bride

Will you be welcoming a new female member to your family through marriage soon? Make her feel welcome by presenting her with a few simple but heartfelt mementos. Have members of the family handwrite some of their famous recipes on cards. On the flip side, tell any stories behind the famous dish. Maybe it is Grandma Lucy's potato salad that was served at every family picnic. Or that pineapple cheesecake Aunt Patty always prepared for Easter dinner.

Another thoughtful gift is to get some small picture frames and place in them wedding pictures of family brides from years gone by. Be sure to also give an empty frame in which the new bride can place her own picture. Then she can display them as a group somewhere in her home.

20.

One for the in-laws and outlaws

If you are married and either of your spouse's parents are still alive, send them a card on Mother's Day or Father's Day, letting them know how very grateful you are for how they raised their child. When I did this for my father-in-law, I specifically pointed out character qualities I see in my husband that I also saw in him. I told him the apple didn't fall far from the tree. It was a very meaningful gesture, and he was touched that I took the time to send it.

21.

Send Dad some secret messages

It's no secret the kiddos are crazy about Dad. Now, tell him! Have members of the family write heartfelt messages to Dad on small strips of paper. These could include memories of special times spent with him or things you love about his personality. Anything goes—just tell him how much he means to you! Then place these warm reminders in various locations where he is sure to find them: his toolbox, the glove compartment, the plastic tote that houses all the Christmas lights he puts up each year, or his backpack or briefcase. All year long, he will unearth these sentimental messages and smile.

22.

The family that camps together . . . has a blast!

No need to hop in the car and venture off to a campground. Set up a tent in the backyard and surprise the kids with an overnight in the outdoors! It will be a special staycation they will remember for years to come.

For supper, serve hot dogs, sweet corn on the grill, barbecued baked beans, and creamy coleslaw. Make a bonfire if you can and toast marshmallows. Sing campfire songs and tell stories or take turns sharing what God has been teaching you lately. Then, tuck everyone in and sleep overnight in the tent.

In the morning, try your hand at cooking something my father-in-law was famous for—biscuits on a stick! Simply purchase some refrigerated biscuits in a tube. Wrap individual biscuits around a stick that is about two inches in diameter. Hold them over a campfire, slowly rotating until they are cooked. (Of course, young children should be supervised at all times near an open fire.) Pair the biscuits with butter, fruit jam, or peanut butter. Best camping breakfast ever!

23.

Start a parent-child or sibling-to-sibling journal

I did this for our daughter when she was in middle school. Purchase a journal to be used between two people as a means of getting to know each other better. Both people take turns asking a question or putting forth a discussion prompter. For example, Mom writes to her daughter, "Tell me your earliest memories of our first home. What did the various rooms look like? What can you remember doing most in each of the rooms? What do you remember about our backyard?"

She then leaves this out for her daughter, who writes several paragraphs giving her answers. Then, before giving it back to Mom, she flips the page and asks her own question, like, "Mom, tell me about when you first met Dad. What specifics can you remember?" She then leaves it out for her mom, who answers and starts the process all over again. The same concept can be used between siblings who are old enough to communicate by written word.

24.

Say it with flowers on a random ordinary day

Do you purchase fresh flowers only for anniversaries, birthdays, or Valentine's Day? Why not celebrate your family life with fresh-cut flowers for any and every reason? Instead of just a few times a year, how about most any time of year? Did your fifth-grader who struggles with his piano lessons just get promoted to a new level book? Did your preteen daughter land a part in the school play? How about the five-year-old who slept at Grandma's all night for the very first time?

This needn't be expensive. It could be that you grab a bouquet at the grocery store on markdown. (Our local market has bouquets regularly on clearance for two to three dollars that still have several days of life left in them!) Be sure to leave a handwritten note with the flowers that says who is being celebrated and why.

25.

Throw a flashback family potluck

All right, this is a supercool way to drum up some nostalgia while whipping up a tasty meal for the extended family. Have all the adult children in the family think back on what dishes they remember the family eating and enjoying when growing up. You may come up with culinary delights such as cheesy potatoes, glorified rice, Mom's famous meat loaf, or even that crazy combination of a lemon-lime Jell-O mold made with shredded carrots and chopped celery!

From this brainstorming session, come up with a menu plan and assign different people to make the various dishes. Then, hold an old-fashioned family potluck to enjoy these entrees and side dishes from years gone by. This is especially fun to do on Grandma and Grandpa's anniversary or a birthday party for the oldest living member of a family.

26.

The five-dollar no-holler date night

My husband and I are always on a quest to go out on fun but inexpensive date nights. We might search for bargain coupons on sites that include local businesses sharing buy-one-get-one-free or percentage-off special offers. Those can really help bring the cost down. An idea that takes a little creativity—but turns out to be loads of fun—is to trek off on a five-dollar date night. Here's how it works:

Use your five dollars to grab a beverage for two at a local eatery. It may be a large chocolate malt, consumed with two straws. Maybe you can score two fruit-flavored iced teas when they are buy-one-get-one-half-off. Then, spend time together just asking questions about life, such as,

- What was your high point of this past week?

- What was your low point of this past week?

- What is one thing you would like to do around the house in the next month?

- What is one place you would like to go with me in the next month or so?

- What is one task I could help you tackle in the next week?

- Is there a particular movie or concert you would like to go to soon? If so, what is it?

- What is your greatest prayer request at work right now?

- What is your greatest prayer request regarding our family right now?

- What is your greatest prayer request in your personal walk with Jesus?

Another fun way to use your five dollars is to give each person $2.50. Then head to a dollar store and split up to do your shopping. Each person must purchase one serious gift for the other with one dollar, and one gag or joke gift with the second dollar. (The remaining fifty cents is to cover the tax.)

Travel to a park or nature center with some food and drink you have brought from home. Eat your food and exchange your gifts, telling why you purchased them. For example, I might buy my husband a new pack of blue ballpoint pens because HE ALWAYS SEEMS TO BE STEALING MINE FROM MY DESK DRAWER! (Oops. Sorry you had to witness my outburst. I feel better now.) Additionally, my husband might buy me a strawberry-flavored lip balm because he remembers me pulling one out of my purse on our very first date. This inexpensive idea forces you to get creative and often brings a smile when the other person sees what you've purchased.

PART THREE

Throughout Your Day and around the Town

Each of us should please our neighbors
for their good, to build them up.

ROMANS 15:2 NIV

Each week brings a new opportunity to
see other people. In your neighborhood.
At the store. At work or in church.
Here are some creative ways to show
these people some love as you go
about your daily routine of life.

Notice the necessary people

My very favorite holiday our family ever celebrated wasn't Christmas or Easter. It was a different holiday—Mr. Brown Day.

Mr. Brown was our mail carrier on the first street we lived on as a family. He was more than just a mail carrier. He was never too busy to chat with a lonely widow or ask a youngster about his Little League game. He was the neighborhood cheerleader. And he was what I like to call a necessary person—someone who faithfully serves us or helps us get life done.

For Mr. Brown Day, our kids purchased a squirt gun for him to use to ward off the neighborhood dogs, and a gift certificate to the local Dairy Queen so he could take Mrs. Brown out for a "fancy dinner." We baked cookies and poured lemonade. Then we hid inside our front door and waited with party blowers and confetti. "Surprise!" we shouted as we threw open the door. "It's Mr. Brown, best mailman in town! Today is officially Mr. Brown Day!" To say he was surprised would be a gross understatement. His heart was truly touched.

Days later, he stood on my porch and declared, "I am still not over Mr. Brown Day." His voice cracking, he continued,

"You know, I have been a mailman on this street for thirty-three years, and no one has ever done anything like what your family did for me. Sure, people remember me at Christmas. But no one has ever reached out to me on a random Tuesday afternoon to say they appreciate what I do. Thank you for Mr. Brown Day."

When we decide to look beyond ourselves—into the faces of others who serve us faithfully all year—we see God. We have an opportunity not only to greet these necessary people face-to-face, but to witness God's very image in them (Genesis 1:27). Brainstorm what necessary person and image bearer you can bless. Here are a few ideas to get you started:

- Leave a cold bottle of water, juice, or soda pop, along with a note of thanks, out for a package delivery person on a hot and humid day.

- On a chilly fall day, take a covered mug of hot cocoa or coffee to a local school crossing guard.

- When going to the doctor, dentist, nail technician, or hair stylist, take along a home-baked treat and a simple note of thanks for their service to you throughout the year.

- Leave a bigger tip than usual for a restaurant server, barista, or other such worker and attach a note of thanks for their faithful service all year long.

- Run a foil-wrapped paper plate of brownies out to the sanitation worker when the collection truck gets to the end of your driveway.

28.

Deliver an "unbirthday" gift

My mother-in-law has the habit of giving what she calls unbirthday gifts. She will often present someone with a little remembrance on a random, ordinary day. In order to be ready in a blink to give an unbirthday present, she sets up what she calls her "General Store" in her basement. There she houses items found on sale or on clearance, such as jewelry, candles, scented lotions, kitchen gadgets, or home décor. Then, when she decides to declare a day someone's unbirthday, she can grab a gift from her stash. Who in your neighborhood or town might need to have an unbirthday soon?

29.

Honoring those who serve

Take some time one day to thank the first responders in your town—law-enforcement officials, ambulance EMTs, and firefighters. Take them a platter of wrapped goodies, such as individual snack cakes, small bags of chips or popcorn, and granola bars. If you have kids, have them draw or paint pictures of these hometown heroes, depicting them in their various roles. Be sure to include a note of appreciation for keeping you safe and being ready to help when troubles arise.

30.

Touch the heart of a teacher

Being a teacher is a hard, and sometimes thankless, job. While I'm sure teachers appreciate the apple-themed trinkets often given to them by their students, here are a few original ideas that are certain to touch their hearts.

> Have your child write a letter to their teacher, in their very best penmanship. In it, have them specifically name three or four things they appreciate about their instructor. Along with the letter, include a gift card to a local coffeehouse in the envelope. Then the teacher can grade homework while sipping on a tasty beverage purchased with the card.

> If you have a child in early elementary school, here's a fun end-of-the-year gift—or even a birthday or Christmas idea. Quiz your student about their favorite things about their teacher and also things about the teacher's looks: What color are her eyes? How old is she? How many years has he been a teacher? What do you love most about her? What do you think he does for fun at home? Then, make up a "test" that has all of the questions on the left-hand side of the paper and all of the answers in random order on the right side. The teacher will need to try to figure out which answers go with which questions. Because of this, make sure you ask several things about colors, numbers, activities,

etc., so the answers aren't so obvious, and be sure to include an answer key on the back. The test usually turns out to be hilarious with some of the answers the students give. Tuck the test in an envelope with a gift certificate for something consumable or a service. Ideas include a pedicure gift certificate or gift card to a local bookstore or café.

31.

Drop off a hug in a mug

Is there a favorite retail worker who seems to go the extra mile? That friendly cashier at the grocery store or the cheerful greeter at the department store who always seems to brighten your day with her encouraging attitude? Choose one of these people and hand-deliver a hug in a mug. Purchase a nice coffee mug, perhaps a pottery one from a local artisan or something whimsical with a fun saying or quote on it. Inside the mug, place some of the following items:

- bags of tea or envelopes of flavored hot cocoas
- some colorful, smooth-writing gel pens
- some old-fashioned candies such as Tootsie Rolls, Jolly Ranchers, Bit-O-Honey, Chuckles, or Pixy Stix
- a trial-sized scented lotion, bubble bath, or perfume
- sticks of smoked sausage or string cheese
- a gift card to a bookstore, miniature golf course, or other appropriate business

Also include some small slips of paper, each one with a written bit of encouragement about the person, such as "You always make my day with your bright smile" or "Your energetic attitude lifts my spirits each time I see you when I enter the store." This hug-in-a-mug recognition for over-the-top efforts on the job will surely be a bright spot in the worker's day.

32.

Refresh a weary road worker

My home state of Michigan is well-known for its seemingly endless road construction in the summer. Slowdowns and detours abound as the workers try to smooth out the roads that are made fragile and full of potholes by the contrast of our hot and humid summers and then bitter-cold winters. Rather than get frustrated when encountering an unexpected stop in a worker zone (which sometimes can last several minutes!), roll down your window and hand out ice-cold bottles of water or flavored teas to the workers, served with a smile and accompanied with your verbal thanks for all their hard work. Kindness in the midst of frustration can change the mood of all involved in no time flat!

33.

Putting their prayers in a basket

Make sure your co-workers know you care about them and are willing to pray for them, should they desire you to. To facilitate this, have either a small basket or a decorative box with a lid on your desk. Near it, place some sticky notes or note cards and a pen. Co-workers may write their prayer requests and place them in the basket or box. Be sure to do this only if your place of employment allows you to.

34.

Document the building of the new neighbor's home

Our neighborhood has a few vacant lots left where people are building new homes and moving into the area from far away. If this is the case for you as well, try this welcoming idea: Take pictures on your phone from the first day they break ground on the new home up until the house is move-in ready. Transfer them onto a flash drive, and then surprise the new neighbors when they move in with the pictorial documentation of their home being constructed. Also, take along a loaf of quick bread or a plate of cookies. (Think, too, about other places where someone new comes on board—the Little League team, dance studio, church, or local school board. Take a baked good or basket of fresh fruit to welcome the new people and make them feel at home.)

35.

Bless 'em in the bleachers

Encourage the fellow soccer, baseball, or football moms and dads on the sidelines at a game or practice. If it is during the cool, fall weather, show up with a thermos of hot cider and some fresh doughnuts to enjoy while you watch your kids play. If the season falls smack-dab in the middle of a blazin' hot summer, try lemonade, iced tea, or even Popsicles instead.

36.

Dish out some welcome as you wait

Store a tote bag in your car that includes items that might be needed should you—and others—find yourselves waiting, perhaps at a sporting event that is delayed due to weather. In this bag, place some protein or whole-grain fruit bars, small bottles of water, bags of nuts or dried fruits, and a couple of crossword puzzle or brainteaser books, along with a few pens. Sure, you could sit and play on your phones, but if preserving the phones' batteries is a concern, you will still have something to do to pass the time.

37.

Create a co-worker sneak-a-snack station

Do you work in an office with co-workers? Be ready in a blink to scatter a little kindness by having a small basket on your desk that will serve as a perpetual stream of treats for any of your co-workers who want to sneak one. Look for after-season sales or clearance bins at the store to purchase individual bags of trail mix, nuts, dried fruits, salty snacks, or candies. (Or maybe try some old-fashioned bubble gum, and you could have a bubble-blowing contest when the boss isn't looking! Shhh.)

38.

Spread a little love
to those at the crossroads

Put together a few individual bags that you can hand out when you see people asking for help at an intersection. Include some protein-packed snacks, such as nuts or meal replacement bars, a gift card to a fast-food chain that is likely within walking distance, a trial-sized package of tissues, some personal hygiene wet wipes, and some confections that will not melt, such as hard mints or fruit-flavored or butterscotch candies. You can also include a booklet with the Gospel of John or a tract that explains the way of salvation through Jesus.

39.

Doing good toward
those who govern

Bless those in your local government or church governing body by taking a platter of goodies to the local school board, church staff or deacon meeting, or city council assembly. You can use store-bought treats or take some time to put together a tray of veggies and dip or a platter of fresh fruit. For a yummy and easy dip to include with the fruit, simply blend together seven ounces of marshmallow fluff and eight ounces of room-temperature cream cheese. Store in the fridge until ready to serve, then let it come to room temperature. So easy but so scrumptious!

PART FOUR

Across the Miles or through the Screen

I hope to see you soon,
and we will talk face to face.

3 JOHN 1:14

At times, we find those we love the most dwell far away. Don't let the distance be a deterrent. You can still show love to those across the miles when you're armed with ideas and a healthy dose of ingenuity. Here are some to get you started.

40.

The ministry of the mailbox

Enact some "ministry of the mailbox." Resurrect the virtually forgotten art of handwriting using paper or note cards. Send a handwritten note of encouragement to a faraway friend or family member, mentioning at least one thing you appreciate most about them. Slip a bag of tea in the envelope for them to enjoy while reading your letter. Those who are homebound or who reside in assisted living are especially grateful for such snail mail.

Or if there is a child in your life who gets overly excited about receiving something in the mail, make it a point to occasionally mail him or her a little surprise, such as a coloring book and pencils or a new joke book. You can even purchase a puzzle and mail just a few adjoining pieces per week. After several trips to the mailbox, the child will have all the components to complete the puzzle.

41.

Share in secret and set off a chain of kindness

Share in secret, also as part of the ministry of the mailbox. It's a breeze! Anonymously mail two five-dollar coffeehouse gift cards to someone, with instructions to use one to treat herself and to give the other away anonymously, paying it forward. Shhh! Don't reveal who started the chain of kindness.

42.

Throw a digital surprise party

Oh, this is a fabulous one! Can't all be together in person to celebrate someone with a surprise birthday, anniversary, or retirement party? You can throw a digital surprise party on Facebook instead. Create a secret Facebook group and invite guests to be a part of it, making sure to tell them not to say anything to the guest of honor. Once the members have joined the group, let them leave their well wishes, sentiments, fun memories, or pictures in the secret group. Then, finally, on the big day, invite the guest of honor to join the group. There they will be able to scroll through to see all the love and happiness in their very own digital surprise party.

43.

Send a cute couple a ten-dollar date night

For the anniversary of a couple you know, mail a ten-dollar date night. Send a card with a ten-dollar bill enclosed. Include a list of questions on some colorful paper. These are designed to initiate conversation on their night out. List questions like, "Tell about the first time you noticed or met each other. What details can you remember?" or "What would be your idea of the perfect getaway weekend just for the two of you?" or "Tell each other the five things you most appreciate about the other's personality." They can then take the questions and the ten dollars and go on a date to enjoy a beverage, split an appetizer, or grab dessert to discuss their questions and answers.

44.

Build a bang-up playlist

Is there a faraway friend or family member who likes to listen to music while exercising? Or perhaps he or she loves to use worship music while spending time alone with God. Or maybe there's someone who has hit a rough time in life and could use some encouragement or even a little relaxation. Utilizing your favorite music app, like Pandora, Spotify, or even YouTube, create a customized playlist just for this person. Then share the list, along with a typed-out prayer for the person, written from your heart.

45.

Scatter some love; sow some seeds

For a friend who has moved away, send a handwritten letter or "thinking of you" greeting card along with a pack of perennial forget-me-not seeds. When they bloom each year, your friend will remember you. Or send a pack of wildflower seeds to your faraway grandchildren or nieces and nephews along with a note that says, "I'm wild about you!" Is there an across-the-country family member who loves to get up early and spend time with God? Send this person a packet of morning glory seeds slipped inside a new devotional book.

46.

Make it a movie night

Gather everything needed to ship a movie night in a box. First, purchase a gift card to an on-demand movie site such as Netflix or Redbox. Inside the box, include microwave movie-theater-style popcorn and old-fashioned movie house candies like Junior Mints, Sugar Babies, Dots, or Whoppers. Include some fuzzy socks or a cozy throw blanket for them to snuggle in as they enjoy the show.

47.

Create a handmade craft fashioned with heartfelt prayers

I have been the recipient of a few lovely gifts that were crafted in the most inspiring way. The first was a hand-thrown pottery mug I received at a conference where I was a guest speaker. It wasn't just special because of the lovely shades of blue and mustard gold that made up the pottery. It was so dear to my heart because the potter who made it spent time praying for me the entire time it was being shaped and fashioned. The event coordinator had given the potter my name and a list of prayer requests based on some things she saw on my social media accounts. Still today, whenever I use that mug, it makes my heart smile. The second such gift was a prayer shawl that was fashioned by several women at a church where I spoke. The women took turns working on crocheting the shawl, and as they did, they prayed for me and my family.

You may not be able to make a mug or crochet a shawl, but you could purchase a craft that you are capable of completing, such as an embroidery piece done with printed canvas or maybe some handmade gift cards. As you work on the craft, pray for the person you will send it to. Then, when you package it up, include a handwritten note mentioning the things you prayed about concerning the person as you made the piece. This handmade craft, fashioned with heartfelt prayers, is sure to speak volumes of love.

48.

Throw an on-screen celebration

Can't get together for a friend or family member's birthday because everyone is scattered across the country—or maybe even across the world? Use an online meeting platform such as Zoom, GoToMeeting, or Teams to throw a virtual party. Everyone can provide their own beverages and food to eat during the bash. Then take turns sharing your greetings and well-wishes to the guest of honor.

You can even play some party games. A simple one is to come up with a list of items they must gather from their homes during a virtual scavenger hunt. Come up with ten categories such as "Something that begins with the letter Q," "Your most unique kitchen utensil," or "Something that was handed down to you." Set a timer for ten minutes. Everyone will dash off to find their items and then return to their screens as fast as possible. Once the time is up, take turns having everyone share the items they gathered and give a digital gift card to the person who got the most items in the quickest time.

49.

Let them eat cake. Or drink coffee!

Is someone across the miles sitting with a loved one at the hospital or even spending time at the bedside of someone passing away in hospice? Find out the address of the medical facility, along with the room number they are in. Then, using a food delivery service, arrange to have a cake, platter of cookies, or other such food sent to the room. (It might be best not to make it a main meal that needs to be kept hot.)

When my own father was in hospice last year, my friend Nicki treated all of the nearly half-dozen family members who were in the room to an assortment of lattes and hot cocoas. It was a little bright spot in an otherwise dark day, and it meant so much to have her perform such a kind gesture even though she lives five states away. You can also do something similar by taking a screenshot of your Starbucks payment code from your app and sending it to them to use to order drinks at their local Starbucks.

50.

Hold a study-and-share summer

For several years, my friend Mary, who lives two states away from me, has joined me for a summer Bible study. Since many women's Bible studies at churches take a break during the summer, we decided to hold a long-distance study with just the two of us.

We took turns each summer choosing a study that we thought both of us would like. Most of them had a format with five days' worth of lessons for each week. We completed the homework on our own during the week. Then each Wednesday morning at seven o'clock, we would jump on the phone to discuss the lessons.

Sometimes there were video sessions that went with the studies. If you decide to do one that does include a video component, you can either both purchase the videos and watch them by yourselves before you meet on the phone, or view it together using FaceTime. If you do this option, make sure that if you purchase the videos digitally rather than on DVD, you purchase them at the group rate, rather than the individual rate.

This summer study will become a time you look forward to each week because not only will you be learning more about God, but you will be discovering more about your long-distance friend, knitting your hearts together as sisters in Christ.

51.

Create a clever wallpaper graphic

A simple idea to brighten the day of a long-distance friend or family member is to make some wallpaper for his or her phone. Locate a picture of the two of you. Using a graphics-editing app such as PicMonkey or Canva, add a Bible verse, favorite quote, or funny saying that is a private joke between the two of you. You can even add a colored background or whimsical border. Make sure you create it in the size intended for a lock screen or home screen of a phone. (The app should have this information for you.) Then email or text your creation to your friend to save and set as the wallpaper on his or her phone. Each time your friend unlocks the phone's screen, he or she will see it and remember you. (Note: You could also use the same apps to make a screensaver for the computer.)

52.

Dig into your past to unearth an impactful person

Using social media, track down a former teacher, church worker, or employer who made a lasting impression on you. Leave a post on this person's wall with a specific memory you have and not only how it impacted you then, but how it has contributed to the person you are today. Thank the person for pouring into your young life. As an added bonus, post a picture you may have of the two of you from back in the day.

PART FIVE

For Those Who Hurt or Need Help

Rejoice with those who rejoice;
weep with those who weep.

ROMANS 12:15

No matter who you are, you are sure
to know someone who is hurting or
in need of help. Whether facing a
grim medical diagnosis, reeling from
the loss of a loved one, or struggling
financially or emotionally, these souls
could benefit from someone taking
the time to stop, notice, and care.
Here are some ways you can be a
bright light in an otherwise gloomy
situation in the life of someone else.

53.

Make their day

My mom has a wonderful perspective about life. Years ago, she taught me that if ever you felt like life was getting you down, you should remind yourself that there's always someone out there who is worse off than you. Go find that person and do something to make his or her day. In some miraculous way, it makes your day as well!

It may be as simple as delivering a fresh doughnut and a hot cup of coffee to the desk of a co-worker going through an unwanted divorce. Or perhaps you take a bouquet of supermarket flowers to the neighbor down the street whose dog just passed away. Could you offer to go get groceries for your elderly neighbor whose back has been bothering her recently? If we just open our eyes, we'll see there are many people around us who could use our helping hand. And helping others helps us to get our eyes off ourselves and realize how many blessings we enjoy every day. So today, think of one person who is in the middle of a not-so-nice situation. Then, go do something to make their day!

54.

Frosty snowman = warmed-up heart

When my children were younger, a fellow mom in our church had a wonderful idea for all of our kids to do one snowy afternoon here in Michigan. We piled the kids in the van and drove to a local nursing home. After asking permission, our children made snowmen on the nursing home lawn, just outside the residents' windows.

We took along some top hats, scarves, and mittens we'd purchased at the local resale shop along with some carrots for the noses. We grabbed some big black buttons for the front of our snowmen (purchased at a local dollar store) and gathered some branches for their arms. This idea is a way to bring a smile to someone else, while also warming your own hearts. It will delight the residents and transport them back to the time when they were young and did the same thing. After the snowmen are all finished, return home and enjoy some hot cocoa.

55.

Gifts for the grieving

Grief is hard. Losing a loved one ushers in a tsunami of sadness. You never know when it is going to hit, something I have learned firsthand after losing both my dad and my sister-in-law recently. Try any one of these ideas to help you comfort someone who is grieving.

One simple gift that was sent to me the very first Christmas after my sister-in-law passed was an ornament for our tree. It was a small metal frame that held a picture of her. My friend Mandy told me to remember the joy Thais had brought to our lives each year when we got the ornament out to decorate for the holidays. In addition to the ornament, Mandy had also written a poem from Thais's perspective about spending her first Christmas in heaven. It was so touching.

Another gift, which hangs proudly on our wall, was a picture our kids special-ordered for my husband after his dad passed away. It shows the position of the stars in the night sky over the exact coordinates where my father-in-law took his last breath. (Try looking on Etsy for such a creative gift.) Underneath the diagram is the verse Isaiah 40:26 (NLT):

> Look up into the heavens. Who created all the stars? He brings them out like an army, one after another, calling each by its name. Because of his great power and incomparable strength, not a single one is missing.

Recently, when one of my son's high school friends passed away very unexpectedly, a friend of mine shipped my son a box of various marinades and barbecue grilling sauces. With it was a card that told him to have his group of friends over for a barbecue so they could reminisce, sharing memories of their classmate.

Finally, one of my close friends was responsible for selling her parents' home after they both left this earth. It was a sad time spent cleaning up the house and donating many of the items inside. A young couple, just starting out building their own family adventure, purchased the house. A few weeks after closing, my friend received a wonderfully thoughtful gift in the mail. When the new owners were remodeling, they stripped off the wallpaper on the dining room wall that had been up for over thirty years. They carefully saved a portion of it and had a heart-shaped piece of it matted in a frame for my friend to hang in her home. That wallpaper had witnessed many Thanksgiving dinners, Easter baskets being opened, and ordinary family dinners with everyone gathered around the dining room table. If you want to do something similar, you could add to the wall hanging the Bible verse 1 Kings 8:57: "May the Lord our God be with us as he was with our ancestors."

56.

Cheer up those spending time with the sick

If people you know have a family member facing an extended illness, they most likely will be spending many hours at the hospital bedside of their loved one. Deliver a basket of love to help sustain them during this trying time. Include some healthy snacks, individually packaged, that they can grab whenever their stomachs start to rumble. Also include some simple prayers and Bible verses written on three-by-five cards—inspirational things to read whenever they are feeling down. My friend Cindy did this once for a family in her neighborhood, and she also included some "childcare coupons" that the family could cash in during one of the many trips made to the hospital. This made it easier for them to ask her to help with their children; they just used a coupon!

57.

When they've lost man's (and woman's) best friend

Losing a pet is rough on all who loved that precious fur baby. A sweet idea to do for someone who is grieving the loss of a pet is to have a local artist paint a canvas picture of the animal. If you can't locate a local artist, try checking an online shop like Etsy. You can also find a picture of the pet on your friend's social media, download it, have a copy made, and then frame it to give to your friend.

58.

Make your move

Moving and setting up house can be a stressful time. Think of ways to lighten the load of those in such a situation. When we moved into our home, my friend Dorothy helped make it so much easier. She showed up with painting supplies in hand and helped us to work on sprucing up a few rooms. She also brought a pot of homemade soup, some store-bought bread, and ice-cream sandwiches for us to enjoy as we took a break. The company and nourishment made this chore so much more pleasant!

59.
Jot that date down!

Here is an idea I came up with several years ago that I use every single year, and it never fails to comfort and encourage someone who is grieving. Whenever I am at a funeral, I make a point to take home the program and take note of the special dates listed inside, such as when the person was born, the day he or she passed away, and an anniversary date if the person was married. Then I record these dates in my paper calendar and also put them in my digital calendar app on my phone. When one of these dates rolls around, I try to think of something to do for the loved ones left behind.

For example, one of my close friends lost her father on a sunny September day. She was very close to her father, and they had a tradition of spending time together on his birthday each April, enjoying a long walk and then some homemade carrot cake. So that first spring without her father, I showed up at her doorstep on what would've been his birthday with a homemade carrot cake in hand. I asked her if she wanted to go for a walk and then enjoy a slice with me. "How did you know?" she asked as she began to cry. I told her it was simple! I had jotted the date down on my calendar.

We also did the same thing for a sweet elderly woman we called Grandma Alma, who had been my children's Sunday school teacher when they were younger. Her husband had passed away. On what would have been their anniversary, my two boys showed up on her doorstep with a bouquet of beautiful yellow roses. They told her that since "Grandpa Don" was in heaven with Jesus now, he couldn't bring her flowers, so he sent them instead. She was so touched and gave them each a big hug.

These days are often difficult for loved ones left behind. When you pop in with a treat or some flowers, you can really help comfort their hearts and cheer their souls.

60.

Give a maxed-out mom the day off

Do you know a maxed-out mom who could use a break? Gift her with a Mom's Day Off basket. First, photocopy the certificate on page 135, and be sure to fill in both her name and your name, along with how to contact you. This certificate announces that she has been given a Mom's Day Off. During a certain set of hours on the day of her choice, her kids will be treated to a day of fun and healthy food while she is treated to a day all by herself. She must agree that on that day she will not do any housework and will do only things she enjoys, such as reading, shopping for herself only, watching a movie, writing letters, or even just taking a nap.

Choose a cute basket or gift bag, and along with the completed certificate, slip in any of the following items, or other items you think she might particularly appreciate.

- a succulent plant in a darling pot
- a bag of flavored coffee or box of fruity herbal tea
- some colorful macarons
- a richly scented candle
- some luxurious lotion or a bottle of bubble bath and a loofah sponge
- a pack of colored pens or pencils and a Scripture coloring book

- a journal, new devotional book, or novel
- a gift card to a local café or eatery
- a new scarf or simple bracelet

The mom you have chosen is instructed on the certificate to get in touch with you to choose the day to redeem her delightful prize. Then your friend will be able to spend the day feeling relaxed and renewed and will rest in the assurance that her kids are being well cared for.

61.

Honor the older generation

If you know of grandparents whose grandchildren live far away and are unable to be with them, have your children adopt them for a day. You could drop by with a snack to share, invite them over for dinner, or take in the local attractions together as you teach your children the importance of honoring their elders. Or take a pretty tea set to the home of a shut-in or elderly friend. Serve tea and muffins and enjoy a leisurely visit. If your young kids are up for it, have them sing songs or play a musical instrument for your friend. Or perhaps you can all watch a movie together and munch on some popcorn as you do.

62.

At your service!

Show up at the home of someone you know who is having trouble keeping up on chores. Rake the leaves, shovel the driveway and sidewalk, weed the flower bed, or wash the windows. Bring a plate of goodies along to share with the person when the work is done. For added fun, you may want to gift your friend with a birdfeeder and a bag of birdseed or a squirrel feeder with some ears of corn, so he or she can enjoy watching some critters in nature long after you are gone.

63.
Take a meal. Do a chore.

Know a new mom with a newborn baby? Sure, take her a meal, but also take along your cleaning bucket too. Clean her house while she and the baby nap. Or tote an empty laundry basket with you. Kidnap her dirty laundry and take it home with you. Wash, dry, and fold it and return a few hours later with her now-clean clothes. There is no tired like newborn tired. This domestic help will be so welcomed!

64.
Throw a "You're finished!" post-treatment party

When a friend or loved one is finished with chemo, radiation, or other such ongoing medical treatment, have a party, complete with all the people he or she loves. Serve some foods the person loves. Have a basket at the party where those in attendance can drop in a card with congratulatory messages or memories of the bravery of the guest of honor while going through treatment. This can be as simple or as elaborate as you want. You can smash a piñata. You can hold it in the summer and have a water balloon fight. Or if it is in the fall, you can light a bonfire and linger around it, visiting and enjoying s'mores or hot dogs roasted over the open flame. The goal is to celebrate that the treatment is complete and your loved one is on the mend.

65.

Love your neighbor as yourself

Have you ever really thought of the concept of loving your neighbor as yourself? It was a somewhat vague concept to me until I began to think about all the ways I make sure that I, myself, am cared for and comfortable. We are so great at loving ourselves, aren't we? We make sure we are fed and clothed, and that we keep warm during the cold months or cool during the sweltering season. We should seek to make sure that other people, especially those on the fringe, are cared for in this same way.

Try this: Choose one way you care for yourself and then schedule a time to care for someone else in this same way. One example might be that you make sure that you have proper hygiene practices. In fact, you love flowery-smelling bubble baths or fruity-scented lotions. Could you scour your community for a shelter for homeless or battered women that is in need of some hygiene products for their residence? Purchase some and deliver them in person, meeting some of the residents if you are allowed to.

PART SIX

Among the Household of Faith

*Now concerning the ministry
to the saints . . .*

2 CORINTHIANS 9:1

As we are spreading the love around,
let's not forget our fellow Jesus
followers in our local church and
beyond. Believers need each other and
are vital to our earthly walk of faith.
Here are some ways you can reach out
and minister to the body of Christ.

66.

Take the Crock-Pot Challenge

When our kids were younger, we had a near-weekly tradition they were so jazzed about. We called it the Crock-Pot Challenge. Curious? Just let your slow cooker do the cooking while you do the inviting. Go to church not knowing whom you will ask home to Sunday dinner, but confident that God has someone in mind for you to share a meal with that day.

I'd make a meat-and-veggies main dish such as beef stew or chicken and wild rice. Then I'd add a simple salad, store-bought bread, and a dessert or ice-cream novelties to round out the meal. You can rotate family members, taking turns with who gets to suggest a person or family each week. Have your kids be on the lookout for someone who had a rough week or could use a little cheering up. Then invite your guests into your home to enjoy the delicious cuisine from your Crock-Pot. It's a sure way to strengthen friendships and make some new ones as well.

67.

Fuel and feed the pastors

As gifts for pastors or others on your church staff, consider sending gas cards to fuel up their cars as they "fuel" the lives of others. Or give them some gift cards for local restaurants where they can take an evening to either go out as a family or grab takeout to enjoy at home. This way you will be feeding them physically as you thank them for feeding your family spiritually all throughout the year.

68.

Siri, whom can I cheer today?

At the beginning of each month, whip out the calendar app on your phone and set an alarm for a day when you don't seem to have a lot going on. Perhaps a Saturday would work best. Set a reminder for that day that says, "Bless a believer!" When you see the reminder pop up, think of a church member who would benefit from a call, a text, or even an invitation for coffee. Or if the person who pops up in your mind is elderly, call to see if he or she needs help with anything that day, such as a ride to the grocery store or some assistance with cleaning the house. You can brighten another believer's day by reaching out with unexpected kindness.

69.
Bake and be ready

How many times have you heard of a family from your church who was in need of a meal and you really wanted to help, but you simply did not have the white space in your day to run to the grocery store, unpack the groceries, whip up a meal, and then take it over to them? Instead of this being the usual routine, be prepared on the front end to bless a person or family in your church with a meal on the day they most need it.

To do so, get ahold of a good freezer cookbook, or find a website that showcases recipes that freeze well. (My favorite online location is the freezer meal section at Allrecipes .com.) Then spend a Saturday morning or afternoon preparing take-and-bake freezer meals that you can easily grab for a new mom, a grieving family, someone who is ill, or anyone who needs a bit of help. I like to try to have a pan of lasagna or a homemade potpie, a frozen fruit salad, and a frozen homemade cheesecake ready to be delivered whenever I hear someone has a need. This way, I only need to swing by the grocery store for a bag of salad and maybe a loaf of bread to complete the meal. Also, be sure to stock up on some note cards or "Thinking of You" greeting cards to deliver along with your meal

70.

Create a set of Scripture tags

Ever have a gift touch your heart and take your breath away? My best friend from college, Kelly, is the most creative gift giver. Over the years, she has stitched, sewn, woven, and spun me many homemade treasures. But one day she outdid herself. She gave me the gift of God's Word. It came in a simple brown-paper-and-twine-wrapped gift with a homemade tag and a handwritten note.

When I opened the package, out fell wonderful pieces of God's heart—handwritten Scripture tags. Each week I randomly choose a new verse to hang on my window over my sink to ponder as I wash yet another glass or scrub a pan or pot.

While it would be easier to type out the verse in a pretty font, Kelly said copying Scripture in her own handwriting helped her to meditate more on the verses because she was physically writing each word.

To do this yourself, purchase some ready-made tags from a craft store. Choose the kind that have strings attached. Or, if you are artsy, make some from card stock and craft paper. Then write out verses that would be particularly relevant to the recipient. Try looking up passages from Psalms, Proverbs, or the Gospels. You might pick a verse or two about God's promises or use BibleGateway.com to look up key words, such as *fear, hope, faith, thankfulness, God's goodness, grace, joy, prayer, perseverance,* etc. Also, praying the Scripture for the person as you write each one out sends even more blessings.

For giving, present them in a small basket, antique jar, or old nostalgic tin. Your friend can pull out a new Scripture tag each time she wants to be encouraged and hang it somewhere she is sure to see it throughout the week.

71.

Let them know they are heaven "scent"

Show your appreciation for a fellow Christian by gifting her with some essential oils and a new oil diffuser, or perhaps a cute candle in an appropriate seasonal scent. (Who doesn't love burning a spiced-apple-cider candle in the fall or a fresh-cut-herbs candle in the spring?) With it, include a handwritten note (or a copy of the ready-made one on page 140) that contains 2 Corinthians 2:14 (ESV): "Thanks be to God, who in Christ always leads us in triumphal procession, and through us spreads the fragrance of the knowledge of him everywhere."

Also, include an encouraging note thanking her for being the fragrance of Christ to everyone around her.

72.

Put on a Prayer Pretzel Party

Years ago, the process of making pretzels was used to teach kids about prayer during Lent. The shape of a traditional pretzel mimics the folding of hands in prayer. Make homemade pretzels as a family, and while they are baking, think of someone from your church who is in need of prayer and spend time talking with God about their need. When the pretzels are done, enjoy some as a family and then wrap up the rest to take to that person, letting them know you are praying for them. If you make a big enough batch, you can take them to multiple people!

Homemade Pretzels

1 cup	very warm water (110°F–115°F)
2 tablespoons	dry yeast (or two packets if using prepackaged instead of bulk)
3 teaspoons + ½ cup	honey, divided
½ cup	butter
1 tablespoon	salt
2½ cups	whole milk
8 cups	whole-wheat white flour (or unbleached flour)
	cooking spray
	butter
	coarse salt

In a large bowl, mix warm water, yeast, and 3 teaspoons honey. Let rest. In a large saucepan, melt butter. Add remaining honey, salt, and milk. Heat this to 120°F over medium heat (use a candy thermometer). Take off stove and let cool 10 minutes. Pour milk mixture into yeast mixture and stir well. Add flour 2 cups at a time. You may need to add a little more or less than 8 cups to make a slightly stiff dough. This depends on the humidity of the day.

Knead dough for 5–10 minutes. Place in a large oiled bowl, cover, and let rise for 1–1½ hours, until doubled in size.

Punch dough down to release air and knead on a lightly floured surface for 5 minutes. Take a piece of dough about the size of a tennis ball. Roll it into a rope about half an inch thick. Make it into a pretzel shape by crossing the ends, leaving about two inches on the ends. Then twist at the intersection of the two ends one time. Fold the ends down to touch the sides, creating a traditional pretzel shape. Repeat with remaining dough. (Makes 10 pretzels on average.)

Place pretzels on a cookie sheet that has been generously sprayed with cooking spray. Bake for 18–20 minutes at 350°F until golden brown. Do not over bake.

When you remove pretzels from the oven, brush them with additional melted butter, then sprinkle coarse salt on top. Serve plain or with mustard or sharp cheddar cheese spread. Enjoy!

73.
Walk with an older saint down memory lane

When I was a junior in high school, our youth group decided to pair up some of the senior saints in our congregation with members of our youth group. Most of these older worshipers had no family nearby. I was assigned Mr. and Mrs. Krieger. They quickly became Grandma Ruby and Grandpa Harold to me.

The reason for this pairing of people was simple: to give the elderly members some company and allow them to share their life lessons with someone younger. I would stop by Grandma and Grandpa Krieger's house just to sit with them and let them chat. Sometimes they told stories of years gone by about our church or our local town. Other times they got out their photo albums and spoke about various seasons in their life together. I was privileged to have them as my adopted grandparents for over a decade until they both passed away.

When their house was being sold and their belongings given away, I was gifted a basket of theirs that was over one hundred years old. I think of them each time I see it sitting on top of my antique Hoosier cupboard. I was also given many of Ruby's canning jars, some with the old-fashioned zinc lids still sporting her cursive handwriting announcing, "Blackberry Jam 1961" or "Stewed Tomatoes 1972."

With the help of someone on your church staff, seek out such an older couple who would love to have instant grandchildren. Make it your simple aim to allow them to reflect on their life as you get to know them. You will be helping to ease their loneliness as you also learn important lessons about life.

74.

Become the church snack lady

Being a staff wife at two different churches taught me very quickly that many ministries of the church often need food. It might be the nursery during the worship services. Or maybe the summer Bible camp held at your church each year. Currently, at my church, it is the college-age group that meets at our on-campus venue at Michigan State University. (Go Green!) I have become known as the snack lady to this group of college students. I keep in contact with the campus director, and he lets me know what is needed for each event. It might be some simple finger foods for a once-a-month weeknight Bible study. Or maybe they need a Crock-Pot of sloppy joes and some soft drinks for a weekend overnight lock-in.

Check with those in charge of the different ministries at your own church to see what food items may be needed. It might not even be that you have to cook or bake. They may just be looking for donations of prepackaged store-bought snacks for the kids and adults. And if homemade goodies are requested, be smart and whip up cookie dough on a day when you have extra time. Freeze it in balls in your freezer so you simply have to bake them on the day they are needed. This is a simple way to serve that enables those in charge to have one less thing to worry about. You, too, can become known as the church snack lady!

75.

Share the good stuff with those who share the Good Word

Galatians 6:6 states, "Let the one who is taught the word share all his good things with the teacher." While most commentators feel it has financial overtones to it—meaning to share your money with those who bring the Word of God—it certainly doesn't need to be limited to that. Why not think of something good to share with the person who teaches the Bible? It may be the person who leads your church or a community Bible study. It might even be a Bible teacher whose studies you attend online or whose written studies and videos you use in your own home. Whoever it is, share something good with this person!

Nose around a little to find out what some of his or her likes and interests are. I once had someone gift me with a basket full of things she'd discovered from my social media that I loved: dark chocolate, coconut-flavored coffee, some vintage Pyrex dishes in my favorite color of aqua, some Ticonderoga number two pencils, and some whimsical note cards.

When giving your gift—no matter how grand or how modest—be sure to share with the recipient something you have learned through his or her teaching that has helped you understand God better or grow closer to Jesus. And include a copy of Galatians 6:6 from page 141.

76.

Deliver a beautiful-feet basket

Here is a unique gift for a Christian friend or worker in the body of Christ—a beautiful feet basket! Grab a darling basket. (I like to scour the secondhand stores or garage sales to find some.) Line it with a fluffy pastel-colored hand towel and place in it several items needed for a pedicure: a pumice stone, foot soak, mint foot lotion, a pedicure foot brush, a few shades of nail polish, and a bottle of clear polish too. You might include a whimsical mug and a bag of her favorite coffee or box of a loved tea. Come to think of it, a few foil-wrapped chocolates wouldn't hurt either!

Handwrite a tag (or use the ready-made one on page 141) that declares, "How beautiful are the feet of those who bring good news" (Romans 10:15). Place the tag in the basket and deliver. So adorable and extremely indulgent.

PART SEVEN

On Holidays, Holy Days, or Just Because

This is the day the Lord has made;
let's rejoice and be glad in it.

PSALM 118:24

A precious widow on the street where I lived when I was first married once told me, "The holidays are an excuse to make someone's life better." Here are some creative ways you can reach out and better someone's life no matter what holiday is at hand.

77.

Encouraging your new friends on New Year's Day

Each New Year's Day, I have a little tradition I've grown to love. While the rest of the family is lounging around watching football or eating leftovers, I grab some note cards and stamps, a warm throw blanket, and a steaming cup of coffee. Then I curl up in front of the fire and think back over the past year that has just come to an end. I single out anyone new that year who has come into my life. It might be a woman who started coming to my church. One year it was the tutor we hired for my son who has dyslexia. Another year, it was the mother of a teammate on my son's travel baseball team.

I take a few moments to pen a short letter to two or three of these people, telling them how thankful to God I am to have met them. Before sealing the envelope, I slip in a single bag of tea. My favorite is from Pukka Tea, and it is actually called Love. It is packaged in a lovely pink wrapper, and the flavor is a blend of chamomile and lavender. This simple New Year's tradition is not only fun for me; I've been told by the recipients of my letters how much it means to them.

78.
Stop letting others be singled out

Let's face it. For many single people, Valentine's Day is the most dreaded day on their calendar. One of my unmarried friends even calls it "Singles Awareness Day." You can help to make this day a wonderful one simply by being purposeful to reach out to someone you know who is unattached romantically.

My husband and I first started doing this a few years back. I recalled how one friend said how much she dreaded seeing the flower delivery person arrive at her office on Valentine's Day. She knew there would be bouquets delivered, but never to her. That gave me an idea.

My husband and I decided not to do anything that cost money on Valentine's Day that year. Instead, we took the money we would've spent for dinner and a movie, or any gifts for each other, and we ordered a single red rose for all of the unattached women who are my co-workers at Proverbs 31 Ministries. It took a little investigating to discover which of the single ladies were not dating anyone. We ordered the flowers to be delivered on Valentine's Day. Each of them had a small gift card attached with a sentiment that read, "You are loved by Jesus and by us."

That morning, my phone started to beep and buzz, alerting me that I had messages. Some of the women cried. One of them admitted she kind of rolled her eyes when she saw the delivery person come into the office, since she was sure none of the flowers were for her. She was happily wrong! My husband and I stayed home that night and ate thin-crust veggie pizza while watching reruns of *Shark Tank*. It was the best Valentine's Day ever.

If you want to expand on this idea, have a bunch of singles over in the evening on Valentine's Day. Set up a taco bar and watch a movie or play a group game. It might become your new favorite holiday tradition.

79.

Gift them a gourmet garden

Okay, this is one of my favorite springtime gifts to deliver to a family with children. First, obtain a new, clean pizza box from a local pizzeria. (Most will just give you one.) Purchase some seed packets that are in keeping with the typical items that normally go into making a pizza: tomatoes, basil, oregano, or marjoram for the sauce; green pepper, onion, or yellow banana pepper for the toppings. Also purchase any assorted gardening accessories you would like to go with the gift. These might include a small trowel, gardening gloves, gardening kneepads, some herb-scented soap, or a watering can.

Tape the seed packets inside the bottom of the pizza box. On the outside, tape a photocopy of the instructions from page 136 that explain what to do with their seed packets. The idea is to prepare a circular plot in the yard. The gardeners will then plant "slices" of the different seeds by dividing the circle into wedges. When the herbs and veggies are ready, they can make a pizza! So fun!

For a scaled-down version of this, gift someone with a salsa garden instead. In two or three quart-sized canning jars, place some starter plants of salsa-related veggies and herbs, such as roma tomatoes, yellow onions, green peppers, jalapeños, or cilantro. Also slip in a copy of my fresh salsa recipe from page 137. When their plants are matured, they can whip up a batch of salsa!

80.
Spring into action

Here are a few springtime surprises to cheer those you love.

- Grab a blanket, go to the discount store, and purchase two kites. Then snatch a friend or family member, stop for some takeout food, and drive to a park with wide-open spaces (watch out for the trees!). Spread your blanket out in the sunshine. Enjoy your food and then fly your kites! When doing this with children, it is fun to return home to watch the classic movie *Mary Poppins*. (Cue the music. . . . "Let's go fly a kite!")

- On the first day of spring, surprise someone with a plate of fresh strawberries disguised as cute carrots. Melt some white dipping chocolate in a double boiler, or over the very lowest setting on your stove top. Squeeze in a few drops each of red and yellow food coloring until it is the desired shade of orange. Dip the strawberries all the way up to the root of the stem and set them on wax paper to harden. (Placing them in the refrigerator for a few minutes will hasten this process.) Ta-da! Most adorable carrots ever! If giving this treat to a child, you might also want to include a stuffed bunny or a copy of any of the Peter Rabbit books by Beatrix Potter.

- Resurrect the habit of celebrating May Day on the first day of that month. Traditionally, small baskets of flowers were anonymously left on the front porch or left dangling from the front doorknob. (Yes, this is one time it is okay to "ding-dong-ditch-it" by ringing the doorbell and then running away!) Older individuals may especially be delighted by this practice since they may remember doing it when they were young children. Include a copy of the tag on page 142 that includes Song of Songs 2:11–13: "For now the winter is past; the rain has ended and gone away. The blossoms appear in the countryside. The time of singing has come."

81.

Write a manuscript of memories

This idea has elicited the most grateful responses! You might not think of yourself as an author, but you can write a manuscript of memories for someone you love. I did this for my mother's seventy-fifth birthday. Our entire family on my husband's side, including adult children and all the grandchildren, did it for his mother when she turned eighty.

Use your computer to type out a list of memories you have of the birthday guy or gal. It can even be short, seemingly random memories. For example, for my mother, I included the time she strapped on my adjustable metal roller skates and proved she could still roller-skate by whirling around the pool table in our basement.

I think it is fun to generate the number of memories that corresponds with what birthday the person is celebrating. For example, "Seventy-Five Memories for Grandma Margaret's Seventy-Fifth" can be the title. Run off the list and place it inside a nice folder with a clear cover purchased from an office supply store. You could also include pages of photographs for more memories to accompany your list.

82.

A loving gift in a loved one's handwriting

A recent gift I gave my daughter-in-law, Macey, was so meaningful to her. Her Southern "Memaw" was famous for making her banana pudding. I reached out to Macey's mother to obtain the handwritten recipe from her grandmother, who'd passed away a few years back. Then I located a shop on Etsy that specializes in transferring handwritten images onto cutting boards. Now my daughter-in-law can see this special piece of the past displayed in her kitchen each time she cooks. And if she wants to, she can whip up a batch of Memaw's famous creamy dessert for my son.

83.

Hold a bicycle parade
for Juneteenth

Juneteenth is combination of the words *June* and *nineteenth*. It commemorates June 19, 1865. That's the day the Union army's Major General Gordon Granger arrived at Galveston, Texas, and informed the slaves of their emancipation from chattel slavery. Give your neighborhood kids something exciting to do to celebrate this holiday by holding story reading time and then putting on a bicycle parade!

First, gather the children and have someone read aloud the book *All Different Now: Juneteenth, the First Day of Freedom* by Angela Johnson (author) and E. B. Lewis (illustrator), making sure they understand what an important day Juneteenth is.

Then venture off to have a celebratory parade. Each child can decorate his or her bike, tricycle, wagon, or skateboard using a variety of objects. While streamers were the old standby, kids can use balloons, shredded metallic paper, and various ribbons. Have a parade route laid out so that older siblings, parents, and neighbors alike can pull out their lawn chairs and take a seat.

Afterward, serve Popsicles or ice-cream sandwiches. You can even award prizes for the most creative or colorful entry. Everyone loves a parade, and we should all love celebrating this crucial day in history.

84.

Warm the heart of a bookworm

Is there a bookworm in your life? Maybe it is a child or even one of the workers from the local library you frequent. August 9 is Book Lovers Day. Take one of the following to your favorite bookworm to celebrate this little-known holiday. Or make up both of the recipes and invite the book lover over for a dinner at your place.

- A pot of dirt pudding, complete with a bookworm or two. This is easy to throw together. Purchase a new plastic flowerpot. If there are holes in the bottom, place a double layer of aluminum foil in the bottom of the pot. Fill it with alternating layers of chocolate and butterscotch pudding and nondairy whipped topping, making sure to finish with a top layer of chocolate pudding. On top of this, sprinkle crushed chocolate cookies. (These can be purchased near the graham cracker crumbs in the supermarket.) Stick a plastic flower—such as a geranium, sunflower, or bouquet of daisies—in the pot. Also include a few gummy worms sticking out of the dirt. Insert a clean gardening trowel for serving. Give with a gardening book.

- Give a Very Veggie Alphabet Soup kit! In a brightly colored gift bag, place the following items: a few chicken bouillon cubes, a 14-ounce can of petite diced tomatoes, a 12-ounce can of tomato paste, a 15-ounce can of lima beans, a 15-ounce can of corn, 3 or 4 potatoes, 2 large carrots, and 1 onion, along with a small box or bag of alphabet-shaped pasta. Include a soup cookbook and a copy of the Very Veggie Alphabet Soup recipe found on page 138.

85.

Squeeze out the last bit
of summer

When those summer days start to fade, squeeze out the
last bit of summer by inviting some friends over to make
the most delicious homemade ice cream you've ever tasted.
This is one of my husband's family's famous recipes. It was
handed down to my mother-in-law, and she continued to
make it with the kids and grandkids in the summer until
she moved into an assisted living facility. This scrumptious
cold confection is called Six Twos. I know, I thought the
name was strange the first time I heard it. It garnered this
title because it has six ingredients, two of each, tossed into
the ice-cream maker.

To make this summery dessert, get an ice-cream maker,
either an electric one or the old-fashioned hand-crank style.
(I can still see my daughter sitting on top of the ice-cream
maker to hold it still while her cousin turned the crank!)

Six Twos

2 cups   full-fat whipping cream

2 cups   half-and-half

2 cups   sugar

juice and pulp from two large lemons

juice and pulp from two large juicing oranges

2   mashed, barely ripe bananas

In the cylinder of the ice-cream maker, place all ingredients. Follow the manufacturer's directions for making your ice cream. I'll bet you've never tasted anything so fruity and refreshing before.

86.

Say it with soup

There's nothing better on a chilly, rainy autumn day than a steaming bowl of bean soup. This yummy gift idea is based on the bean soup that is served daily in the United States Senate restaurant.* You might even want to give it to someone on Election Day in November—maybe even to someone you know is politically the polar opposite of you!

In a quart canning jar, place two pounds of dried navy beans. Place a new plaid dishcloth in a fall color scheme over the lid and secure with a rubber band. Include both a copy of the Senate Bean Soup recipe from page 139 and the gift tag from page 142 with Joel 2:23 (NIV), "Rejoice in the Lord your God, for he has given you the autumn rains because he is faithful." Punch a hole in each of the tags, thread a piece of jute twine through them, and tie around the jar, over the rubber band.

Steaming soup will be good for their soul. (Note: You can always make the soup yourself and give that in a quart canning jar with a lid. Then you'd only need to attach the Scripture tag.)

*"Senate Bean Soup," United States Senate, accessed September 9, 2020, https://www.cop.senate.gov/reference/reference_item/bean_soup.htm.

87.

Give your Thanksgiving some international flair

Use Thanksgiving as an opportunity to reach out to someone from another culture. It's a sad fact that many international students studying in the United States are here for four or more years yet never see the inside of an American home.

Contact your local college, specifically the international student office. See if there are any students who are going to be alone at Thanksgiving. Contact them and invite them to your family's feast.

We did this once with a man from China. Our children were very small at the time, but they loved visiting with him and asking him questions about his culture. He taught them to eat with chopsticks. He tasted cranberries and stuffing for the very first time. When we dropped him back at his dormitory, he could hardly talk because he was so emotional when expressing his gratitude for our inviting him into our family that day. If we hadn't, he probably would have eaten something cold out of a can in his dorm room, since he did not have any way to heat up his food and the dorm cafeteria was closed. It was so effortless on our part to run over to the university to get him for the day, but the gesture spoke volumes of love to him.

88.

Do you wanna build a snowman? (Or maybe make a scarecrow?)

This gift idea will inspire some fun memories as the recipients either build a snowman or construct a scarecrow with the contents of the gift. Simply gather all the things needed to make a snowman—a top hat, a scarf, a pair of mittens, some sticks for arms, some big black buttons, and don't forget a corncob pipe! You can either include an artificial carrot from a craft store or instruct the recipient to grab a carrot from the fridge when it's time to make the snowman come to life.

In the fall, do the same thing, but for the construction of a scarecrow. Include a flannel shirt, an old pair of jeans, some work boots purchased secondhand, a straw hat, and an old pillowcase with a few permanent markers for drawing a face. Deliver it, along with a bale of hay, and let the scarecrow building begin! These kits are especially fun for families with young children.

Pull off a top-secret Twelve Days of Christmas

One year, a close friend of ours went through an unwanted divorce that left him all alone, in a new tiny house, with his five children. When the beginning of December rolled around, my husband and I got a phone call from him. He was standing in the middle of a home improvement store, trying to pick out a Christmas tree and some inexpensive ornaments. He was trying his best to give his children some semblance of normal at Christmas. We quickly hopped in the car and went to the store to help him. He was fighting back the tears, and it just about broke my heart in two. But it also gave me a great idea.

When I got back home, I emailed eleven other families from our church and community who I knew adored this man and his sweet children. I invited them to help pull off a Twelve Days of Christmas Surprises caper. All of them agreed and, oh boy, was this a blast!

First, I found a huge market basket at a resale shop. Then, on the first day of Christmas (traditionally the Twelve Days of Christmas starts December 25 and ends January 5, but I started December 13 so the final day would be Christmas Eve), the market basket appeared on their doorstep at the crack of dawn before anyone there was awake. In it, my husband and I had placed a homemade chicken potpie, some peanut butter apple crisp, a bag of salad and a bottle of dressing, a new board game, some Christmas lights and decorations, along with a small envelope for each child with a five-dollar gift card to the local discount store. We included a handwritten note that said, "Surprise! It is the first day of Christmas! Enjoy your dinner, put up your decorations, play a board game as a family, and pick out a new trinket or toy for each child. You are loved!" We did not sign our name. In the note, they were also instructed to put the empty basket back on the porch before going to bed.

Each of the remaining days of Christmas, miraculously before dawn, the basket was refilled again with another note written anonymously from yet another family. Sometimes there was homemade food. Other times there were gift certificates to a local pizzeria or Chinese restaurant. There were handmade items. Soccer balls and jump ropes. Sometimes there were new mittens and hats for the children. Each day was different and as delightful as the one before.

Our friend asked me if I knew anything about who was behind it. (Of course, I didn't spill the beans!) He said it was such a lifesaver for him and for his children. It generated excitement each night as they went to bed, wondering what they would find in the basket the next morning. It was a great way to share God's love and to help a family through a very difficult time emotionally.

90.

Participate in the Great Doughnut Drop

The church my mother attends in her town has a marvelous idea I just have to share. Each Christmas Eve, the church sets up a table in the entryway filled with boxes of doughnuts purchased from a local bakery. After the early evening service, church members grab a box of doughnuts along with a slip of paper with an address to a location around town. These locations are all businesses or government buildings where people are working on Christmas Eve, such as fire departments, police stations, the ambulance barn, hospitals, and walk-in clinics. They then pile into their vehicles and pull off the great doughnut drop, delivering the decadent pastries, along with some smiles, to those who must work on Christmas Eve. The members of the church, especially the children, look forward to doing this every year.

PART EIGHT

By Opening
Your Home

He brought them into his house,
set a meal before them, and rejoiced.

ACTS 16:34

There is no better location for showing
love to others than right there in
your own four walls. Here are some
ways your home can become a center
of encouragement for others.

91.

Provide a personal retreat

Offer to provide your home as a personal retreat for a friend in need of some quiet time. (You might have to volunteer to babysit her children at her house in order to make it happen.)

Give your friend a key to your house and let her come steal away for a day. Stock your fridge and cupboard with snacks. Leave a little gift basket with items such as a journal and pen, a new coffee mug, a book you think she would enjoy, or a warm knitted throw blanket to snuggle up in. Then, she can spend her day any way she wishes. She might want to watch movies or do research on the Internet. She may want to take a nap or read a book. The key is that she won't be tempted to clean out a junk drawer or fold laundry since she isn't in her own home.

92.

Lights! Camera! Action!

During a seasonable time of year, host a backyard movie night. To do this, rent or borrow a projector that plays DVDs or projects the contents of your smart TV onto a screen. Rig up a movie screen by hanging a white sheet from two ladders, some trees, or even a clothesline. Offer popcorn and beverages for your guests, and also some bug spray to ward off mosquitoes. Provide blankets or lawn chairs for everyone to sit on. Then let the show begin as you enjoy a memorable time taking in a movie right there in the great outdoors.

93.

Hold a vintage-skill class

Millennials and members of Generation Z are showing increased interest in learning old-fashioned homemaking methods, such as knitting or crocheting or how to can green beans.

If you are skilled at such a vintage procedure, consider holding a free class for those who are not. Over the years, I've taught a few members of the younger generation how to make a flaky piecrust, how to preserve homemade salsa, or how to transform a few flats of fresh strawberries into freezer jam. For a little remembrance of the day, you can even send them home with some handwritten recipe cards or a new book that takes them further along in the skill.

94.

Plan a Parents' Day Off

For the brave only! If you know of several couples who are in the thick of raising young children, gift them with a Parents' Day Off by opening up your home to serve as a childcare center for a few (or several) hours one Saturday. This is especially helpful during November and December, when the parents may want to go Christmas shopping without the little ones in tow.

Provide some crafts and appropriate movies to keep the kids busy. Serve them a healthy snack, or even an entire meal, if they will be there during a mealtime. You could even try your hand at letting them bake and decorate a platter of Christmas cookies to give to their parents when they are picked up at the end of their time with you. This will ensure that these slightly stressed-out parents get a little break, and also have a chunk of time to get some things done without having to also watch their children.

95.
Be our guest! Be our guest!

Overnight company coming? Create a welcome basket for them. Fill it with trial-sized bottles of shampoo and conditioner. Add a handful of chocolates. Tip: After major holidays, many stores mark down foil-wrapped seasonal chocolates, sometimes up to 90 percent off. Grab a bag or two that are wrapped in a generic way, perhaps in gold, silver, or red foil. Other items to be on the lookout for: granola bars, single-use beauty face masks, disposable razors, cotton swabs, trial-sized bottles of mouthwash or tubes of toothpaste, and colorful washcloths that you can roll up and tie with a lace ribbon.

96.

Left over but not left out

I have a friend who has a weekly tradition I think is so resourceful. It is common knowledge among her circle of friends that they have a standing invitation on Sunday evenings to bring their favorite board game and any leftovers they have over to her house. They then set up a buffet with all of the food, adding in a few bags of salad or some store-bought cookies or brownies if needed.

This idea is so clever because someone else's leftovers don't seem left over to you. If you're tired of eating chicken and noodles for the past two days, but you spy a half pan of lasagna at the smorgasbord now set out in front of you, it just might whet your appetite. Your gang can eat and play board games while the children hang out together watching a movie or playing in the backyard.

97.

Present an international buffet

Do you have a co-worker who is of a different nationality? Did new neighbors just move into your development who were born and raised in a foreign land? Do your homework and figure out what type of cuisine is native to their homelands. Then invite them and their family over for dinner one night and serve them that ethnic offering.

Making it your intention to enter their world not only speaks volumes of love to them but also broadens your horizons! I have tasted all sorts of delicacies from different countries, listened to music I never would have been exposed to, and learned about various sports and hobbies in which I had no previous interest. But I have to admit, it all was rather fun! (My favorite is discovering fresh-roasted Ethiopian coffee!) Purpose today to enter the worlds of others—and discover a whole new world yourself!

98.

Throw a My Favorite Things party

No raindrops on roses or kitten whiskers needed. My friend Nicki did this once, and it was a total hit! For a delightful gathering, host a My Favorite Things party. You provide some light refreshments and a coffee bar with creamers and sugar. Each of your invited guests chooses a favorite item of hers that costs less than five dollars. It might be a kitchen gadget, a fantastic set of smooth-gliding gel pens, or a personal-sized hand sanitizer that smells heavenly.

Each guest purchases five of her favorite thing, wraps them individually, and brings them to the party. Designate a table for guests to place their items, and also have a basket, some slips of paper, and pens. Each guest writes her name on five slips of paper and drops them in the basket.

Then the excitement begins! Each person takes a turn telling the group all about her item and why it is one of her favorite things. Then she draws five names out of the basket, and each of those guests gets to take home one of the items just described. Finish by enjoying your snacks and beverages.

99.

Small home? Tiny budget? No big deal!

If you feel like you don't have a large enough home—or a hefty budget to match it—consider having others over but hosting them outside and asking them to provide part of the meal.

You might hold an old-fashioned ice-cream social. You provide the ice cream, either store-bought or hand-cranked. Guests bring various toppings. Or try a baked potato bar. Make several large baked potatoes wrapped in foil. Keep them warm in a slow cooker set on low. Have guests bring various toppings, such as steamed broccoli, sautéed mushrooms, taco meat, shredded cheeses, bacon bits, sour cream, and pizza sauce with chopped pepperoni. Add a simple drink and home-made cookies for dessert. And enjoy your meal outside if the weather is nice.

100.
Cram for exams

If you have a finished basement or other suitable space in your home, such as a large family room or an open living room/dining room floor plan, invite some college students over the week of exams.

Provide them with plenty of space to spread out at various tables and desks, or by utilizing lapboards on couches or chairs. Even beanbag chairs work fine. Have them bring along their homework, any devices they may need, and a set of earphones. Supply them with a steady stream of munchies along with a refrigerator stocked with soft drinks or a self-serve coffee bar.

Allow them to study alone, or perhaps study in pairs quizzing each other if they have the same class. You might even want to allow them to pull an all-nighter and finish up your time together by feeding them a hot breakfast. They will surely appreciate the space to study, along with the tasty food. It will be a welcome change from staring at the four walls of their dorm rooms while they try to concentrate.

101.
Host a Mug and Muffin

For nearly a decade, my friend Carmen and I put on a once-a-month gathering in either her home or mine that grew to be known as Mug and Muffin. The concept is simple. You provide the home, along with everything to have coffee, tea, or even hot cocoa or hot spiced cider in the cold months. Have two to three people sign up to bring a dozen muffins each, depending on how many people you have attending. (We started out with about a dozen, and by the time we were finished, we had nearly ninety people on the mailing list!)

The night of Mug and Muffin, everyone brings her favorite mug and five dollars. Guests enjoy a hot beverage and some yummy muffins. Use the five dollars to pay a speaker to come present to your group. It could be somebody who actually speaks for a living. Or it just might be someone from your church or circle of friends who has an area of expertise. We had presenters speak on taking great pictures of your kids, how to start an herb garden, how to decorate for the holidays on a shoestring, and much more. Or you might just want to have an older (or older in the faith) woman share a mentoring message with the group. It's a great way to give women a night out, learn a new skill or spiritual lesson, and provide an avenue for making new friends.

Printables

Choose-a-Chore
Coupon

Congratulations! You are the proud recipient of this Chose-a-Chore coupon. On one of the dates you suggest, you will be given a helping hand with any chore of your choosing. It can be tackling some deep cleaning, painting a room, gutting out your garage, weeding the garden, or reorganizing your kitchen. Anything goes!

To claim your prize,
text the code "FREE HELP"
to _____

Please include the chore you need help with, as well as a few possible dates for redeeming your coupon. We can then set a date on the calendar for your free time of help.

Offer expires _____.

Signed,

_____

It's a
Sorta-Spa
Party!

Then Jesus said, "Let's go off by ourselves
to a quiet place and rest awhile."

Mark 6:31 NLT

You are cordially invited to a time designed
to help you relax and unwind.
No need to bring anything, except for yourself.
Our goal will be to spend time having facials,
polishing our fingernails, and enjoying some light
refreshments and a time of prayer.

I hope you can join us!

Date: _____

Time: _____

Address: _____

RVSP by _____ to _____

Signed: _____

Sourdough Bread Recipe

½ cup	sourdough starter, room temperature
¾ cup	warm (110°F–115°F) purified or spring water (do not use tap water)
3 cups	unbleached bread flour, divided
¼ cup	corn oil
1¼ teaspoons	salt
	cooking spray

Pour starter into a large mixing bowl. Add the warm water, 1½ cups of flour, and corn oil. Beat for one minute with a wooden spoon. Cover with plastic wrap and set it aside for 4–6 hours.

Add the salt and the remaining flour, a little at a time. Knead on a floured board for 5 minutes, until the dough is smooth and elastic, adding more flour if needed. Place the dough in a large, greased bowl. Spray the top with cooking oil spray and cover the bowl with plastic wrap. Let rise until doubled, about 1 to 2 hours.

Punch down dough and divide in half. Shape each half into a round loaf and place on a lightly greased, cornmeal-sprinkled baking sheet or pizza stone. Lightly spray with cooking spray. Cover loosely with a clean dish towel and let rise until doubled, about 2 hours. Remove the cover, score the top with a sharp knife, and bake at 425°F for 20 minutes or until lightly golden brown. Let cool on a cooling rack before slicing.

Mom's
Day Off

Congratulations!
You have earned a Mom's Day Off!

On the day of your choosing, between the hours of
_____ and _____, your kids will be loved, cared
for, and properly fed while you enjoy some time off
from the important job of motherhood.

During your day off, you may engage in any of the
activities you find relaxing or enjoyable. Go shopping
for yourself. Take in a movie. Go for a leisurely stroll
in a park. Curl up on the couch and read a book. Or
even take a long, uninterrupted nap. Anything that will
refresh and rejuvenate you.

To claim your prize and select the date on which you
will redeem it, please text "MAXED-OUT MOM" to
_____. You will receive a call back within
twenty-four hours to set up your much-needed day off.

Offer expires _____.

Signed,

_____

Plant a
Pizza Garden!

Use the enclosed seed packets
to plant a pizza garden!

Simply prepare a circular plot in the ground.
(You may want to mix in some rich store-bought
garden soil along with your existing dirt.)
Section off wedges of the circle and plant "slices"
of each of the plants included in this box.

When the plants are ready, harvest them
and create a delicious pizza.

Enjoy!

Fresh Garden Salsa

6	Roma tomatoes, cored and diced
3	fresh jalapeño peppers, seeded and chopped
1	medium yellow onion, chopped
2	cloves garlic, peeled and crushed
3 tablespoons	chopped fresh cilantro leaves
2 tablespoons	fresh lime juice
2 tablespoons	fresh lemon juice
1½ teaspoons	ground cumin
1 (10 ounce) can	diced tomatoes with green chilies, drained
½ teaspoon	salt
¼ teaspoon	ground black pepper

Place all ingredients in a bowl. Toss gently to mix well. Cover and store in the refrigerator at least two hours before serving. Serve with crisp tortilla chips. Makes about 8 cups.

Very Veggie Alphabet Soup

Chop the onion and potatoes and peel and thinly slice the carrots. In a large kettle or stockpot, sauté these in 2–3 tablespoons of vegetable oil for 5 minutes. Sprinkle with some salt and pepper and add all of the cans of veggies, undrained, along with the tomato paste. Add 6 cups of water and the bouillon cubes. Simmer, uncovered, over medium-low heat for an hour. Add 1 cup alphabet pasta and cook 30 minutes longer. If needed, add more salt and pepper to taste, and serve. Serves 8–10.

Senate Bean Soup

2 pounds	dried navy beans
4 quarts	hot water
1½ pounds	smoked ham hocks (may use 2½ cups chopped cooked ham instead)
1	onion, chopped
2 tablespoons	butter
	salt and pepper to taste

Rinse beans with hot water. Place beans in a large pot with 4 quarts hot water. Add ham hocks (or chopped ham) and simmer over low heat for approximately 3 hours in a covered pot, stirring occasionally. If using ham hocks, remove them and set aside to cool. Dice meat and return to soup. Lightly brown the onion in butter. Add to soup. Before serving, bring to a boil and season with salt and pepper. Serves 8.

Pursue the Lord
and his strength;
seek his face *always*!

PSALM 105:4 CEB

Thanks be to God,
who in Christ *always* leads us
in triumphal procession, and through
us *spreads* the fragrance of the
knowledge of him *everywhere.*

2 CORINTHIANS 2:14 ESV

Let the one who is taught the word share all his *good things* with the teacher.

GALATIANS 6:6 CSB

How *beautiful* are the feet of those who bring *good news.*

ROMANS 10:15 CSB

For now the *winter* is past; the *rain* has ended and gone away. The *blossoms* appear in the countryside. The time of *singing* has come.

SONG OF SONGS 2:11-13 CSB

Rejoice in the Lord your God, for he has given you the *autumn* rains because he is *faithful.*

JOEL 2:23 NIV

KAREN EHMAN is a *New York Times* bestselling author, a Proverbs 31 Ministries speaker, and a writer for *Encouragement for Today*, an online devotional that reaches more than four million women daily. She has written sixteen books and Bible studies and is a contributing writer at the First 5 Bible study app. Karen has been featured on numerous media outlets, including *TODAY* Show Parents, FoxNews.com, Redbook .com, Crosswalk.com, and *HomeLife* magazine. Her passion is to help women live their priorities as they reflect the gospel to a watching world. Married to her college sweetheart, Todd, she is the mother of three and mother-in-law of two, and she enjoys collecting vintage kitchenware, cheering for the Detroit Tigers, and feeding the many people who gather around her mid-century dining room table for a taste of Mama Karen's cooking. Connect with her at karenehman.com.

Proverbs 31
MINISTRIES

Know the Truth. Live the Truth. It changes everything.

If you were inspired by Karen Ehman's *Make Their Day* and desire to deepen your own personal relationship with Jesus Christ, Proverbs 31 Ministries has just what you are looking for. Proverbs 31 Ministries exists to be a trusted friend who will take you by the hand and walk by your side, leading you one step closer to the heart of God through

- free online daily devotions
- First 5 Bible study app
- online Bible studies
- podcast
- COMPEL Writer Training
- She Speaks Conference
- books and resources

Our desire is to help you to know the Truth and live the Truth. Because when you do, it changes everything.

For more information about Proverbs 31 Ministries,
visit www.Proverbs31.org.